COYOTES

Sandie Lee Books

Coyotes

This animal is in the canine family. The coyote is also known as, the American jackal. This animal is very smart and has learned to live with its habitat loss. The coyote has also been depicted in many Native American, Aboriginal and First Nation's myths and stories. The coyote is usually shown as a cunning and clever animal. If you think this is interesting, check out some cool facts on the coyote. Read on to discover more...

Where in the World?

Did you know the coyote can be found as far north as Alaska? The coyote has made its range all over the world. It can be found throughout North and Central America, from Panama and throughout Mexico. It can also be found in many places in the United States and Canada.

The Body of a Coyote

Did you know the coyote looks similar to some dog species? This animal has a pointed snout, a flat forehead and pointed ears. It can measure up to 37 inches long for males and weigh up to 50 pounds. It can reach heights of 20 inches at the shoulder. Females will be slightly smaller.

The Coyote's Coat

Did you know this mammal has a thick coat? The fur of a coyote is grizzled in appearance. It can be anywhere from greyish-brown to reddish-brown. This animal has a thick undercoat to keep it warm in the winter. The coyote has been heavily hunted for its pelt for use in human clothing.

What a Coyote Eats

Did you know the coyote is considered an, opportunistic feeder? This means the coyote will eat what it can, when it can - even if the prey is already dead. The main diet of this species of animal includes small mammals, fish, fruit, insects, livestock and even larger animals like deer.

The Coyote's Special Ability

Did you know the coyote can run very fast?
This animal can reach speeds of up to 40
miles-per-hour for short distances. This makes
it one of the fastest land animals in North
America. The coyote's own territory can range
from a few miles up to 62 square miles.

The Coyote's Senses

Did you know this animal has a strong sense of smell and hearing? The nose and ears of a coyote is its most important sense. This animal can detect hunters and other predators from miles away. The coyote can even hear a small rodent scurrying under the snow.

The Coyote as a Predator

Did you know the coyote stalks its prey? The coyote will hunt small prey from up to 164 feet away. When it is ready, the coyote will make a quick dash or a hard pounce onto its live food. This animal will also hunt as a pack to take down larger game.

The Helpful Hunter

Did you know coyotes are helpful in keeping the rodent population down? In some areas, the coyote is welcomed as it keeps the pesky rodent population under control. This animal has also been known to help out the American badger. The coyote sniffs out an animal in its burrow and the badger runs into it and chases the animal out.

The Coyote as Prey

Did you know this animal is hunted by other animals? Even though the coyote is usually safe in its pack, some animals will hunt the very young, weak or old coyote. These include the mountain lion, bears and wolves. Man has hunted the coyote for its pelt and also because they view it as a nuisance animal.

Coyote Talk

Did you know this mammal can make lots of sounds? The calls of the coyote can range from yips, yelps, barks and even howling. These can be long drawn-out calls or short notes. The coyote is most likely to make sounds in the early evening and at night or during the mating season

The Coyote Mom

Did you know the mother coyote makes a den for her babies? The female coyote will get pregnant between January and March of each year. She can have up to 19 pups! But the average is only six. The pups will nurse milk from their mother until they are old enough to eat meat.

The Coyote Baby

Do you know the baby coyote is called, a pup? The coyote pup only weighs about 0.5 of a pound when it is born. Its eyes are closed and its ears are floppy. After 3 weeks the pup will leave the den for short exploring sessions. By 12 weeks-old, the pup is learning the skills it will need to hunt.

Coyotes at Play

Did you know coyotes will chase and play with each other? Like dogs, coyotes will engage in play fights, running and wrestling with each other. Coyotes can also wag their tails. This is done when greeting another coyote. This animal's tail will rotate in a circular motion or in a slow back-and-forth motion.

Life of a Coyote

Did you know coyotes can live up to 18 years in captivity? Since coyotes are hunted by man and other animals, so many do not make it to adulthood. If a coyote is healthy and left alone by predators, it could live to be 10 years-old in the wild. Coyotes that live in and around rural areas, run the risk of being hit by a car, or killed by man.

Quiz

Question 1: What other name is the coyote known by?

Answer 1: The American jackal

Question 2: What has the coyote been heavily hunted for?

Answer 2: Its coat

Question 3: What other animal does the coyote hunt with?

Answer 3: The badger

Question 4: Like a dog what can a coyote do?

Answer 4: Wag its tail

Question 5: How long can a coyote live in captivity

Answer 5: It can live up 18 years-old

Thank you for checking out another addition from Sandie Lee Books! Make sure to check out Amazon.com for many other great titles.

www.ingramcontent.com/pod-product-compliance
Lightning Source LLC
Chambersburg PA
CBHW050801290526
45792CB00008B/2273